Confidence Looks Good on You

Exchange the Lie for the Truth of Who You are in Christ

Susan Vandenheuvel

This book is dedicated to, first and fore-most, my Lord and Savior, Jesus Christ, without Whose tender love and work in my life I would not be writing this book.

Secondly, I'd like to acknowledge my wonderful husband, Tim, who has been a constant source of encouragement, love, and support. Not only in this endeavor but throughout our more than twenty-five years together, you have been a living ex-ample of the love and grace of God. You believed in me even when I didn't believe in myself. You and I alone know the tremen-dous sacrifice you've made so that I can pursue God's calling in my life. I love you.

Finally, to my beautiful daughter, Sam. May you always know you are a daughter of the King; you are His! May you always be confident in who He says you are! May His voice be the loudest in your life! And may you always know just how over the moon I am about you! (PS: And may your ears always be open to hear Mom in your ear, telling you, "Get the Thin Mints!")
Choose (You)•nique!

Contents

Introduction

THERE'S A STOLEN-IDENTITY crisis in our world, only the stakes are much higher than social security numbers, bank accounts, and demographic information. All over the world, there are women who don't know who they are in Christ. These are women who are sitting next to us in the church pew and singing in the choir. They can be women who teach Sunday school and lead us in worship.

These are women walking through life wounded, wearing a mantle of shame, regret, rejection, and insecurity. Jesus said in John 8:32, "You shall know the truth, and the truth shall set you free." The truth is that you are not whatever it is you've done in your past; you're not the mistakes you've made or the label someone has put on you. The truth is that you are the righteousness of Christ Who dwells in you; you have been chosen, redeemed, forgiven. The truth is that you are highly loved and have incredible worth and value. Above any-thing else and before any other title you wear, you are a daughter of the King of kings!

How do I know? Because I was that woman, and I've met countless others who once wore that same mantle. When Jesus said the truth would set us free, He was referring to His truth, the truth found in the Bible. The truth of how He sees us, sees our lives and future, the truth of the thoughts He thinks about us is the truth that sets us free and gives us confidence.

It is my deepest prayer that each person who picks up this book will find true and lasting freedom by exchanging the lies for the truth. May you hear Jesus singing this over you:

> *I will change your name*
> *You shall no longer be called*
> *Wounded, outcast, lonely, or afraid*
> *I will change your name*
> *Your new name shall be*
> *Confidence, joyfulness, overcoming one*
> *Faithfulness, friend of God*
> *One who seeks My face*

> —Lyrics by D. J. Butler © 1987 Mercy/
> Vineyard Publishing

Believing in and for each of you,
Susan

She Rises *victoriously*
because He bore her defeat

She Rises *forgiven*
because He bore her sin

She Rises *loved*
because He first loved her

She Rises *chosen*
because He bore her rejection

She Rises *fearless*
because His love is greater

She Rises *unashamed*
because He bore her shame

She Rises *redeemed*
because He ransomed her

She Rises *purposeful*
because He has a plan for her life

She Rises *unshaken*
because He said she's more than a conqueror

She *Rises*
because He first rose

1
A Confident Heart

Have no confidence in the flesh.

—Phil. 3:3

CONFIDENT. *THE AMERICAN College Dictionary* defines confident as "having a strong belief or full assurance; sure: confident of victory." It goes on to describe confident as "being sure of oneself; bold." The word *oneself* stood out to me when I read this definition. Many of us, myself included, have tried a wide variety of things in hopes of gaining even a small measure of confidence. I wonder if you, like me, are tired of trying those things—whatever those things are—only to be let down and succumb to insecurity.

We don't want to admit it, but insecurity often drives the ways in which we respond to certain situations and in relationships. It's sort of like something lurking within us that we want desperately to rid ourselves of, but like a pesky fly at a summer picnic, it just seems to be ever present, annoying us at every turn. Everyone wants to feel confident—an honest confidence that helps carry ourselves well and helps us engage in conversation feeling like we have something to offer. Confidence that, while not being arrogant, gives us the freedom to be true to ourselves and to stop falling victim to someone's opinion of us, decisions we've made and later regretted, or even our own self-destructive patterns.

Titles, college degrees, status, club memberships, bank accounts, and the latest fashions hanging in our closets are just a few of the ways we try to gain confidence. Having these things isn't bad; it's when the things we possess have *us* that we get out of balance. When we need things to feel confident or to give us a measure of worth and value, those things will eventually leave us feeling disappointed and empty. Much like an addict needing to increase his or her habit, what once gave us a sense of worth and value eventually fades, leaving us to begin the search all over again. There are countless people in the sports and entertainment industries that were once well known for their achievements but as life would have it somehow become a memory. Soon a younger version emerges, someone who is faster on the racetrack, throws the ball farther, sings better, or acts better on the big screen. It would be easy to find one's identity in who "I was." The thing that trips us up is that eventually those things fade, leaving us asking, "Who am I...really?"

It's such a draining cycle, a cycle I'm convinced doesn't bring freedom or the very thing we so desperately want: a confident heart. Think about it. A confident heart. What would that look like to you? I spent so many years desperately yearning for it. It always seemed like it could be reality for others, but somehow it couldn't be my reality. Like a bone that a dog tied to a fence post can see but can't get to, a confident heart just seemed so far out of reach. I was bound to my past and not only what I thought others thought of me but what I thought of myself.

Twenty-two years ago, I gave my heart to Jesus Christ. I came to Him in my brokenness, with a heart full of hurt and disappointment after disappointment. When I heard of the love of God and what His Son, Jesus, did for me and that I could be free from the mistakes I had made (there were plenty, let me tell you) through asking for forgiveness, my heart was overwhelmed. By the time I gave my heart to Christ, I was in my early twenties and had a lot of regret. Although according to God I was forgiven (1 John 1:9) and according to His Word, I was a new creation (2 Cor. 5:17), I just didn't *feel* free from my past and the regret I carried. I continued in the same self-destructive patterns. I would read the truth found in Scripture, hear wonderful messages, read inspiring books, and ask others to pray with me, but I just couldn't seem to be free from myself. My thoughts about myself, my life, and the future just didn't align with what I was reading and hearing.

Insecurity and a lack of confidence are a result of not fully understanding who we are *in* Christ. Self-confidence isn't what sets us free from the exhausting search for a confident heart. The things in this world will never give us true worth and value. At the end of the day, those things are just that: things. They don't have the power to sustain us when what I refer to as blasts from the past flood our memories. Philippians 3:3 tells us, "Have no confidence in the flesh." My struggle with moving from the past to the present and seeing myself, my life, and my future through His eyes rather than mine stemmed from not fully understanding first who I belonged to. Isaiah 43:1 says:

> But now, thus says the Lord, who created you, O Jacob, and He who formed you, O Israel; "Fear not, for I have redeemed you; I have called you by your name; you are Mine."

He said I belonged to Him. He called me as His own. He actually *wanted* to claim me. There's a freedom that comes from a revelation of that truth. It's more than a mere download of information that gets stuck in our minds; it's an understanding that settles and dwells in the very fiber of our being.

So, we're not after a deeper revelation of what self-confidence looks like because it's not self-confidence that sets us free. We're after a confidence that says no matter what, success or failure, approval or none, another's opinion of us—title or no title, educated or not—I *know* who I belong to and who I am in Christ.

Does the thought of no longer being identified by your past but by what God says sound too good to be true? I know! Trust me, I get it! It sort of messes with our minds, doesn't it? Somehow our brains just can't seem to wrap themselves around the truth that we don't have to be defined by our past but by what He says.

Romans 12:2 reads, in part, "be renewed by the transforming of your mind." It takes time to see this change take place, but it is fully possible, even for you! No one is exempt from living with a confident heart. Anyone can apply the truth of Scripture and see a trans-formation in thoughts, heart, and life! It will require a commitment to study and an activation of one's faith to believe what the Word of God says. Second Corinthians 5:7 puts it this way: "we walk by faith, not by sight."

As we apply this Scripture to what we're talking about in this book, we can live a life of faith by confidently choosing to believe what the Word of God says, placing our faith in what and who He says we are, not what someone else says we are or aren't.

By not following our feelings or thoughts, we'll grow more and more confident in our hearts. To see you and me walking in complete confidence that we belong to Christ and that He has given us our identity is God's heart for every person on the face of the planet.

Because my ministry is mainly focused toward women, I will address this battle of insecurity from a woman's perspective. However, I must say that the words contained within this book can be applied to men as well. Insecurity and the need for a sense of worth and value are not gender issues. They cross gender lines as well as ethnicities, socioeconomic lines, and even different cultures. Every person was created to know his or her worth and value in Christ and to live life with a confident heart in that understanding.

The percentage of women who engage in some sort of self-shaming talk in any given week is astounding. I'm sure you've heard it at your workplace, family gatherings, and at the ladies' night out. Maybe you've even engaged in the conversation about yourself. I know I have. I've been the one that started the conversation, exposing my thoughts to friends and family alike. Conversations that centered on how inferior I felt to someone and how I could never do "that" (whatever "that" was) because "she" was better than me.

Women especially have a tendency to compare themselves with one another. When a woman walks into the room, we measure her up and sadly determine, based on how she looks, whether or not we think we could be friends. Is she dressed better than me? Thinner? Is every hair in its place? And the ever-dreaded, seemingly effortless way she makes friends makes us feel even more inadequate. Forget that she's a kind and compassionate and humble person—that ol' insecurity is rearing its nasty head again. Have you been there? Me too! The irony is that the very thing we see in her is what we're yearning for.

Would you like to walk in the confidence of who God says you are, with your shoulders back, head up, and engaging those around you with authenticity? I want authentic relationships that allow me to be me— the *real* me. I don't want to have to pretend or try to impress others. I want to be confident in who I am, the way God created me.

What if we as women could be at a place of freedom and full confidence that even though you and I don't look alike or share the same gifts, we could still appreciate one another by celebrating our uniqueness? What if the gifts we see in another didn't leave us feeling inferior or threatened? What if we no longer felt like we needed to make another look bad in the eyes of our friends, simply because what she possessed was different from what we did? What if we could give genuine compliments to another with the pure motive of building her up in her unique gifts? What if we surrounded ourselves with not just those who are like us but those who are not? What if we welcomed the creativity and unique gifts of another to the group, even if it's "not the way we've done it before"?

Every woman wants to be confident—so much so that she'll go do a variety of things to get it, even some extreme methods. From extreme diets, saying yes when the answer should be no (and vice versa), to addictions, insecurity affects every area of our lives. It affects the decisions we make, our relationships, how we see ourselves, our lives, and our futures. A lack of confidence weighs us down and makes us feel lowly. A lack of confidence even affects how we approach God in prayer and worship. No one else may see it, but we are fully aware it's there; we just get good at keeping it stuffed.

When I look back at some of the decisions I've made, the ones I later regretted, I see plainly they were made from a lack of confidence. Wanting to please people, I've said yes (or no) to questions because I knew that's what they wanted to hear. I've agreed to go places because I wasn't confident in standing firm in my personal convictions. Like many women, I've struggled not to fall prey to fitting into the culture's "mold" in an effort to be accepted. Every woman knows the struggle is real!

It's as if there's a heavy yoke around our necks that keeps us from standing upright and living life confidently. But when a woman knows who she is in Christ, she begins to rise from that position and walk in confidence. One of my favorite verses in the Bible is found in Isaiah 61:3: "To all who mourn in Israel, He will give a crown of beauty for ashes, a joyous bless-ing instead of mourning, festive praise instead of despair" (NLT).

A crown of beauty for ashes. In Christ we can rise from the ash heap and be fully alive! We can choose to live victorious instead of with a defeated mind-set. Isn't that some great news?

Maybe you've picked up this book because the title caught your eye. Confidence. You would admit (even if it's under your breath!), "Yes, I'd like to be fully clothed in confidence." So, how do we get there? We all want more, but how? How does it happen? Before we can see this confident heart affecting every area of our lives, something needs to change *within* us. We can't give away something we don't have. Our thoughts—how we see ourselves, our lives, futures, gifts, and unique-ness—have to change.

Friend, if I were sitting with you, I'd pull up closer and look at you and tell you how beautiful you are and how much potential you have. I'd tell you God has such wonderful plans for you and has created you with a purpose (see Jer. 29:11). I'd grab your hand and say I believe in you. I'd tell you what I see in you. I'd tell you how loved you are, and then I'd ask you to put down the lens you've been viewing yourself through and begin to see yourself through the eyes of your Creator. I'd reassure you that God is fully trustworthy and will gently take you off this cycle of self-shaming talk and show you your worth and value in Him.

I don't know what you've been through, and I don't know your story. I don't know what words have been spoken to you that have caused deep wounds in your heart. I don't know what you're currently thinking, feeling, or going through. But what I do know and am fully convinced of is that Jesus sees you. You are on His mind. In the previous paragraph, I shared the things I'd say to you if we were together. God wants to help you come to a place in your heart that, even if I hadn't said those things, you'll be completely confident that He does.

I was on a prayer retreat recently that was located in a wooded area. I ventured out each day for a walk on the unpaved trails and to talk with Jesus. I feel so close to Him when I'm in that element. One particular day I had ventured farther out, and I came to a place where I needed to make a decision to go right or go left.

Admittedly, I am directionally challenged. (I can see my husband nodding his head and saying, "Yes, you are.") When I'm driving somewhere unfamiliar, I need landmarks to help navigate my route. I can't seem to follow directions of north, south, east, and west. I need directions like, "Turn right at the blue house" (and hope whoever lives there will never repaint the house!).

So, while I was standing on that trail contemplating my decision, I knew I would need to be able to find my way back. As silly as it sounds, I needed to use wisdom! My ability to find my way hinged on that decision.

Many of us have a deep desire to be free from insecurity. We want to live confidently and embrace life to its fullest, believing God's truth. We want so desperately to believe what we read of our identity in Christ to be for "me" too.

So many women are standing at a fork in the road, contemplating a decision: to go all in and finally be set free from whatever keeps them living in freedom, or to continue down the same ol' path. Unfortunately, familiarity often wins the day. Even when the same ol' way of living isn't fulfilling and leaves us feeling empty, many of us will stay the course because we've gotten comfortable with it. We can, after all, adapt. It's what is normal.

In an effort to help you choose the best way, the way of freedom and victory, I'd like you to picture yourself standing there trying to decide. Then you look up and see street signs: to the left, Defeated Road, and to the right, Victory Lane.

Today can be a new day! Your decision will be a defining one. Let me be your cheerleader! Hear me shouting, "This way!"

Girlfriend, point your toes to the right! Victory is down this way!

Oh, and by the way, Jesus is cheering you on too!

2
A Timeless Story

*Now Laban had two daughters. The
older daughter was named Leah, and the
younger one was Rachel.*

—Gen. 29:16

I LOVE THAT the people we read about in the
Bible were real people who had things to overcome.
Somehow it's reassuring that the things that seem to
be an Achilles' heel in my life were also experienced
in their lives. Life can leave us feeling like we're walking around with an invisible target on our backs. Have
you ever felt like you went from one fiery furnace to
another?

I remember being new to my faith and attending a Bible study with twelve "seasoned" women who were much further along in their faith. Each week I attended, I learned something that helped me grow in my faith and made me love Jesus even more. One week in particular, I had a deeper understanding that those people we had been reading about weren't perfect. Maybe you never wondered how you would ever live like those in the Bible, but I did! I would read of their stories, and somehow I missed their shortcomings. Instead I saw them as strong, faithful followers of Christ who never wavered in their faith but were quite loyal. That Tuesday morning seated around the table and discovering the opposite was true was a defining moment in my faith.

I'm not saying the lives of those we read of weren't strong, faithful believers, but those people did have things to overcome, just like the rest of us. To someone who struggled with perfectionism, learning this was life changing! While those seated around that table didn't need that revelation, God knew I did, and it changed my perspective in a major way.

Some time ago, God began speaking to my heart about confidence and led me to the story of Leah and Rachel. Maybe you're familiar with these two sisters. They had classic insecurities, and boy did they have sibling rivalry! I can only imagine being in the same house as these two! Their story is the all-too-familiar clamoring for attention by trying to outdo the other. I think it's interesting how many years ago this story is recorded, and yet here we are in 2016, and the struggle remains! Time comes and goes, but some things women have had to overcome are timeless. Maybe their story isn't directly like yours, but the signs, effects, and motives can still be seen.

I think there's such wisdom in laying a foundation for any story one begins to study. I have to believe there are women newer to their faith who have found this book in their hands. For the sake of those not as familiar with Leah and Rachel, would you allow me space to lay a foundation for us? Maybe as you who are more seasoned in your faith read their story, something new and fresh will bounce off the page at you, or maybe you'll be reminded of a point in their story that will help you as we go on. Regardless of where you find yourself in your faith, let's get a glimpse into the background of Leah and Rachel. Their story can be found on the pages of Genesis 29:16–30.

> *Now Laban had two daughters. The older daughter was named Leah, and the younger one was Rachel. There was no sparkle in Leah's eyes, but Rachel had a beautiful figure and a lovely face. Since Jacob was in love with Rachel, he told her father, "I'll work for you*

for seven years if you'll give me Rachel, your younger daughter, as my wife."

"Agreed!" Laban replied. "I'd rather give her to you than to anyone else. Stay and work with me." So Jacob worked seven years to pay for Rachel. But his love for her was so strong that it seemed to him but a few days.

Finally, the time came for him to marry her. "I have fulfilled my agreement," Jacob said to Laban. "Now give me my wife so I can sleep with her."

So Laban invited everyone in the neighborhood and prepared a wedding feast. But that night, when it was dark, Laban took Leah to Jacob, and he slept with her. (Laban had given Leah a servant, Zilpah, to be her maid.)

But when Jacob woke up in the morning— it was Leah! "What have you done to me?" Jacob raged at Laban. "I worked seven years for Rachel! Why have you tricked me?"

"It's not our custom here to marry off a younger daughter ahead of the firstborn," Laban replied. "But wait until the bridal week is over; then we'll give you Rachel, too—provided you promise to work another seven years for me."

So Jacob agreed to work seven more years. A week after Jacob had married Leah, Laban *gave him Rachel, too. (Laban gave Rachel a servant, Bilhah, to be her maid.) So Jacob slept with Rachel, too, and he loved her much more than Leah. He then stayed and worked for Laban the additional seven years.*

Did you catch it? Jacob loved Rachel and worked for her but was tricked! Laban gave him Leah instead of Rachel. As we read this story, one would wonder how this could have happened; how could they have had such close contact with one another and Jacob not know he was with Leah? Then Jacob worked another seven years for Rachel. If you're anything like me, you're reading that and seeing trouble written all over the tent in which they dwelled! Two wives only equals one thing—*trouble*! It was the culture's way, especially if the first wife was barren. Jacob worked seven years for Rachel but instead got Leah. Then Jacob worked another seven years for Rachel.

Can someone say, "He's just not that into you?"

Imagine. Laban is a manipulator, Jacob feels totally duped, Leah feels like she's playing second fiddle, and Rachel must've been wondering what on earth was going on. My, my, my, what a story! Doesn't this sound like a reality show you'd find while channel surfing? But, there it is, written for us in Scripture. I wonder if you've ever felt duped or played second fiddle. Like I said earlier, the names are maybe different, but the story is timeless.

I can only imagine what Leah must have been feeling. If she were to let you and me into her thoughts, I wonder if we would hear this: "I'm not good enough. I'm not pretty enough. Somehow, I just don't measure up." I wonder if the question "What does Rachel have that I don't?" consumed her every waking moment. Have you had these thoughts? Can you add a few yourself? I wonder if these thoughts had been replayed in her head, just like programming your favorite song to replay over and over. Scripture doesn't tell us, but it does lead one to wonder.

Rachel, Rachel, Rachel! (Said in the tone of "Marsha, Marsha, Marsha!" from the old sitcom, *The Brady Bunch*). It's always about Rachel.

Leah, it seemed, lived in the shadow of her sister. I wonder if, when Jacob came on the scene, Leah felt she would finally step out from that shadow and be her own woman. Her own identity. Her life. Then she had to share Jacob with her sister. Can you imagine? Actions spoke loudly that Leah wasn't as loved as Rachel. Leah was indeed the lesser-loved wife. All throughout her story, Leah strived for worth, value, confidence, and love. It's still the story all these years later for countless women. The methods we use may not be what we'll see that Leah used, but the striving continues.

Bring on the Babies

Shortly after being given to Jacob, Leah began having children. As you will soon see, this only brought more rivalry between Leah and Rachel. However, in chapter six, you will also read how God brought something wonderful through the birth of Leah's fourth son, Judah.

As in any victory God works out in our lives, there's a "going through" phase. While Leah was giving birth naturally to children, God was birthing something *within* her that could only be done by experiencing Him in the depths of her pain. It's no different for you and me. It's human nature to try to avoid feelings of discomfort, but that's impossible, simply because we live in a fallen world. Having gone through many things myself, I can say I am grateful for what I've learned, how I've grown, and what I've discovered about God. The things I've had to endure have allowed me to lean into Him and have given me a more intimate relationship with Him.

I want to encourage you if you're currently going through something. Psalm 23:4 reads, "Yea, though I walk through the valley." You may be in a dark valley where the day seems like night. Reread that verse. Jesus hasn't left your side. Keep walking, putting one foot in front of the other. There's another side to what you're facing. Keep your eye on Jesus and your hand in His. You are going to make it to the other side.

Maybe as you read this book, stuffed emotions will begin to rise. Something will resonate with your story, and it won't leave you feeling warm and fuzzy. If we were still sitting with one another, I'd move from my chair and sit next to you. I'd put my arm around you and believe with you that God will give you the strength you need to keep going, to keep pressing in so that you can have a confident heart. It has been a prayer of mine as I've written this book that you will feel God giving you the courage you need and that you will sense Him making you brave to move from where you are into freedom.

Power can be misplaced. Have you given power to something other than Jesus? Who or what is ruling your thoughts, feelings, choices, and behaviors? I'm believing for you that you will find the courage to take the power given to your past and give it instead to Jesus Christ and what He says about you.

Genesis 29:31–35 tells us of the sons Leah gave birth to:

> *When the Lord saw that Leah was unloved, He enabled her to have children, but Rachel could not conceive. So Leah became pregnant and gave birth to a son. She named him Reuben, for she said, "The Lord has noticed my misery, and now my husband will love me."*

> *She soon became pregnant again and gave birth to another son. She named him Simeon, for she said, "The LORD heard that I was unloved and has given me another son."*
>
> *Then she became pregnant a third time and gave birth to another son. He was named Levi, for she said, "Surely this time my husband will feel affection for me, since I have given him three sons!"*
>
> *Once again Leah became pregnant and gave birth to another son. She named him Judah, for she said, "Now I will praise the LORD!" And then she stopped having children.*

Let's take a closer look at verse thirty-four: *Then she became pregnant a third time and gave birth to another son. He was named Levi, for she said, "Surely this time my husband will feel affection for me, since I have given him three sons."* Can you hear her desperation? "Surely this time…" In other words, can you detect in her thoughts that she's given her husband not one, not two, but *three* sons? Not only is she up three to zero in the sibling rivalry, but she's given her husband not girls but boys. Male children were considered a blessing, as they would carry on the family name and have a great place in society.

Leah must have thought Jacob would certainly notice her, esteem her, and see her value and worth. I also find it interesting that with the first child, Leah says, "Now my husband will love me." It seems that after the birth of her first three children Leah's hope had waned. From *now* to *surely*. Surely gives a hint of "maybe this time," as if Leah was speculating within herself.

Disappointment would once again rule the day, as Jacob failed to meet Leah's expectations. Isn't that the way it goes? What have you tried (or are you currently trying) in hopes of gaining the attention of someone you deem special or significant? What have you tried (or are you currently trying) in an effort to gain even a morsel of confidence? Is disappointment ruling your day? Has your hope waned?

Striving only produces one thing: frustration. That is, until we think of something new that we haven't tried before. Then we go into "this is it" mode, only to see disappointment rule once again. It's such a cruel cycle. There is hope, however, and you can step off the merry-go-round and begin living life confidently.

Who is *Your* Jacob?

Before we start unpacking this timeless story in the next four chapters, I wanted to make a special point about one of the main characters in this story—Jacob.

While this story is one of two sisters sharing the same husband, you'll notice that it really focuses on the relationship between Leah and Jacob.

I don't want anyone to be confused that Jacob only represents our husbands. Far from it. Just because Jacob was the source of much anguish in Leah's life, let's not lose perspective. First, as you will see in the following chapters, God used this situation to develop within Leah something pretty incredible. Secondly, Jacob can represent anyone in your life who makes you feel worthless, diminished in some way, less than, unloved, or condemned—anyone who makes you feel shame or rejects you for some reason.

Be sure to keep that in front of you as you start turning the pages of this book!

3
He Sees You

The Lord looks from heaven; He sees.

—Ps. 33:13

WITH THE BIRTH of each child, Leah hoped to secure Jacob's affection and love, only to be left feeling disappointed. We're no different. As we discovered earlier, we try quite a few things to become more confident. We buy the lie that tells us, "If I do this, I'll feel better about myself and finally have the confidence I have been looking for."

What is it that you think would make you feel more confident? You know, that one thing?

There's nothing wrong with having desires. I often encourage people that God places desires within our hearts and that if you "delight yourself in the Lord, He'll give you the desires of your heart" (Ps. 37:4). I am fully convinced that we serve a big God and that we are created to believe big, dream big, and pray big. The catch is when the things we desire have *us* instead of the other way around.

We are to delight ourselves *in Him*, not in things, desires, or even our dreams. Our relationship with God isn't a priority, He *is* the priority! He should come before anything we desire and before any earthly relationship.

Leah wanted Jacob to be a one-woman man. I want Tim to be a one-woman man. If you read Genesis 30, you'll read Rachel lamenting to Jacob that she wanted children. Tim and I wanted to have a child. There's nothing wrong with desires. But take any two women, and one will feel a lack in something. If we don't know who we are in Christ and we don't guard our hearts, something so silly and innocent can turn into envy and jealousy because one wants what she doesn't have. We become deceived into thinking if we had that one thing we would finally be confident.

God wants us to become so confident in who we are in Him that we stop the comparing and competing with one another. What if we stopped buying the lie? What if we stopped taking the baited trap from the enemy and instead appreciated one another? What if we could cheer one another on in our gifts? What if we did it genuinely? What if you could recognize that God created you uniquely and be confident that, even though someone may be different than you, it doesn't make you any less significant?

I am fully convinced that when we as sisters in Christ do these things and link arms with one another in unity, we will see a greater impact in our spheres of influence.

Three Names/Three Meanings

In the culture in which Leah and Rachel lived, great thought was given to what to name children. If you were to study the names of children as they were born, you'll see the newborns' names had meaning. The name often had something to do with the child's future, the situation in which the child was born, or even the mother's thoughts and feelings at the time of birth.

Today, there is much thought given to what we'll name our children, but I'm not sure it has the significance it had in biblical times. There are many books available in an effort to help moms and dads pick that perfect name. Nowadays, one can research what the most popular names are currently. It seems in our present day, unique wins the day. We even like to make the spelling of names unique.

For instance, my name is spelled Susan. I've seen my name spelled Suzan, and while one would assume that spelling would sound like the name Suzanne, it doesn't. Both are pronounced the same. Being someone who likes uniqueness, I sort of like the unique spelling of my name, using the letter *z*. When I was young, I found this spelling and tried to use it in school. The teacher wasn't as supportive of my desire to display my uniqueness when I needed to put my name on my homework. So, Susan it was, with an *s*.

Beginning with this chapter, we're going to pull apart the names of Leah's children to see the meanings behind each. As you'll discover, she named each with a purpose that reflected where she was in her thoughts and feelings. Following the study of each name, I'm going to offer you a few Scripture verses that will help you discover truth.

I wonder if you'll see yourself in these meanings of the names given to Leah's sons. Maybe you'll see yourself in just one; others may identify with all the names. Wherever you find yourself, please be encouraged that you're not alone. Identifying yourself with these meanings in no way means you're a bad person or silly or just need to "get over it."

From the beginning of time, there has been a very real enemy that has had one goal for God's daughters. In John 10:10 Jesus said, "The thief does not come except to steal, and to kill, and to destroy. I have come that they may have life, and that they may have it more abundantly." Satan, our enemy, wants to discourage you, diminish you, fill your mind with lies, steal your joy, destroy any hopes you may have of being fully confident and free from fears and insecurities, and kill any life within you, even if it's just a flicker.

There is freedom and hope! It's found in the truth of Jesus Christ and what He said He came to give all humanity. For you. For me. You are not somehow exempt from being completely free and confident in your identity in Christ. Before we go any further, pause where you are and pray a simple prayer. Ask the Lord to help you believe that the life He came to give us is meant for you too. Invite the Holy Spirit to help you apply the truth to your thoughts, feelings, and faith.

The first son Leah gave birth to she named Reuben. Reuben means "See, a son." Although Jacob may not have "seen" his wife, Scripture says God saw her. God noticed her. Leah was never lost from God's view. He never had a bad view, as if something were in His way and He couldn't see around it. He knew exactly where she was at every moment of every day. I wonder how many times Leah felt unnoticed by her husband. There she sat across the table from him, lay next to him in their bed, walked with him, but he never "noticed."

In my opinion, Jacob's lack of noticing Leah began the first night they spent together. How could he not notice he was with Leah?

Unnoticed. Like a wallflower, blending into the crowd, nothing really noteworthy or significant. Often when people feel unnoticed, they will try things to draw attention. Would this describe you? Are you tempted to be a "yes man" (or "yes woman"), agreeing to do something in an effort to be seen, even though you know it will compromise your convictions? Do you feel tempted to dress in a way that's a little less modest and makes *you* feel uncomfortable?

We live in a culture where "skin is in" (or out, depending on how you want to use the phrase). We can't escape it; it's everywhere from the local grocery store to, dare I even say, the church. It grieves my heart when I see women and young girls wearing clothing that reveals parts of their body that should be kept for that special someone. Rather than judging these beautiful daughters of God, I cannot escape thinking that they don't know their true value and worth in Him. If women and young girls truly knew this value and worth, they wouldn't dress in a way that draws attention—the wrong attention.

Perhaps you would admit that you try to work harder to gain the attention of those in upper management or the guy sitting in the cubicle next to you.

After all, you're weary of always being the bridesmaid but never the bride. Do the hours you keep at your workplace stem from the workload, or is there another motive? Be assured that God sees your commitment to your job and notices how hard you've worked on that project. He also notices when someone else gets the credit for your hard work. He notices the disappointment that comes from consistently being overlooked.

Rest assured that because He is for you and sees you, He will bring you to a place (even if it's not physically) within yourself that confidently knows He is your Rewarder. And when God honors you, it will not only be the right timing, but it will also be in a way that means so much more than anything someone in your office could have done for you.

Women have also gone to great lengths to be more beautiful to garner the attention of others. Please hear me: I am in no way suggesting taking care of ourselves is a sin or demonstrates a weakness within you. I like having great hair! When I feel like I'm having a great day in the hair department of life, it just puts an extra skip in my step! I love going to the salon for a color. I try to eat right, get plenty of rest, and drink plenty of water.

What I'm trying to communicate is that there's a difference between desiring a healthy lifestyle and feeling like we *need* to have these things before we can be confident. In other words, somehow our identity is found *in* these things. I don't think God opposes these things, but He wants us to keep a healthy perspective.

Just as God saw Leah, He sees *you*! *You* are on His radar. All over the planet, people are calling upon His name, and yet He sees—notices—you, right where you are. Right now. At this very moment. But don't just take my word for it; let God share His heart with you:

> *When I consider Your heavens, the work of Your fingers, the moon and the stars which You have ordained, what is man that You are mindful of him, and the son of man that you visit him?*
>
> —Ps. 8:3–4

> *The Lord looks from heaven; He sees all the sons of men.*
>
> —Ps. 33:13

As you read these Scriptures and the others I've included in this book, please don't be confused when you read words that might suggest the promises of God are gender-specific. Be confident in applying these promises to you! These verses promise that God sees *you*.

4

He Hears You

But God did listen! He paid attention to
my prayer.

—Ps. 66:19

LEAH'S SECOND SON was named Simeon. His
name means "heard; to hear." Jacob may not have heard
Leah's voice, but God not only heard her voice—I am
convinced He also heard her heart.

Scripture says God "heard she was unloved." It makes
me wonder how He heard that. What were the conversations like between Leah and Jacob that God could
hear she was unloved? What were the conversations

like between Jacob and Rachel that God could hear Leah was unloved? Words, or the lack of them, say a lot about how one feels toward another.

I'm sure you, like me, have been in a room where the comments made about someone led you to believe the person in question wasn't too loved. Sadly, I've been in a room where a husband and wife were in conversation, and it was pretty obvious one of them wasn't being heard, giving way to feelings of being unloved.

When I read Leah's story, I wonder if in those conversations with Jacob she asked, "Could you tell me what I might do to win your affection? Would you be willing to give me the same amount of attention as I see and hear you give Rachel? If only you…" What did Leah *hear*?

Remember we read that Jacob loved Rachel. Women especially have a need to feel loved. It's more than a love language, as much as that is relevant. Love is our greatest need; it's what we long for. These feelings of being loved aren't met solely by the words others say but are felt and have a greater meaning when those words are followed by an active demonstration of what's being said. Women feel loved when care, loyalty, quality time, openness, and esteem are demonstrated.

On the other hand, when women wonder where (or if) we fall on the priority list, if secrets are kept, and if we are the constant brunt of jokes in the presence of others, women will feel unloved. If our man is constantly remarking about the woman at the office or looking a little longer at the woman across the room than he ought to, it leaves us feeling insecure of his loyalty toward us.

There's not enough space within this book—and in all honesty it's probably best saved for another title—but if pornography is brought into the home...major heartache. Mercy! Women spend enough time comparing ourselves with others. We don't need any help!

What do you do to be heard? Do you feel everyone has a voice but you? When in a gathering, do you want to contribute but then change your mind because what you would say just seems silly? Do you wonder if there's really anything you could contribute to conversations? Have you ever had the experience of being in a conversation (using that term loosely here) that's so one-sided you couldn't get a word in? How about those experiences of constantly being talked over and interrupted?

Maybe you'd admit that this is you and that you've been tempted to talk this way or that way to fit in. You know, use bigger words to impress others. Or you've been tempted to throw in a few slang words that are offensive to the Holy Spirit within you, but it's how everyone at the office talks. Have you ever wanted so badly to be a part of a conversation, to feel included, that you tried talking about a subject you weren't really knowledgeable in? That's embarrassing.

Have you ever wanted to beg someone, "Please just listen to my heart"?

Just as God heard Leah, He hears *you*! God said if you call upon Him, He'll answer you; if you cry out to Him, He'll hear you. God gives you His *full* and *undivided* attention. He hears your heart and actually loves the sound of your voice! He'll never grow tired of you or roll His eyes when you come to Him. As you read these promises of God, it is my prayer for you that you'll become confident that He hears you!

> *The Lord has heard my plea; the Lord will answer my prayer.*
>
> *—Ps. 6:9 (NLT)*

> *I have called upon You, for You will hear me, O God; incline Your ear to me and hear my speech.*
>
> *—Ps. 17:6*

> *But God did listen! He paid attention to my prayer. Praise God, who did not ignore my prayer or withdraw His unfailing love from me.*
>
> *—Ps. 66:19–20 (NLT)*

There's another story of a woman I bet would have been a good friend to Leah. Her name is Hannah, and her story is found in 1 Samuel. While there are striking similarities between Leah's and Hannah's stories, unlike Leah, Hannah was unable to have children, and that was viewed then as a curse from God. Hannah's husband also had another wife, Peninnah. Scripture records that Peninnah had many children. First Samuel 1:4 reads, "And whenever the time came for Elkanah to make an offering, he would give portions to Peninnah his wife and to *all* her sons and daughters" (emphasis mine).

A bit further in that same chapter, Hannah is found praying this prayer:

> *And she was in bitterness of soul, and prayed to the LORD and wept in anguish. Then she made a vow and said, "O LORD of hosts, if You will indeed look on the affliction of Your maidservant and remember me, and not forget Your maidservant, but will give Your maidservant a male child, then I will give him to the LORD all the days of his life, and no razor shall come upon his head."*
>
> *And it happened, as she continued praying before the LORD, that Eli watched her mouth. Now Hannah spoke in her heart; only her lips*

> *moved, but her voice was not heard. Therefore*
> *Eli thought she was drunk. So Eli said to her,*
> *"How long will you be drunk? Put your wine*
> *away from you!"*
>
> *But Hannah answered and said, "No, my*
> *lord, I am a woman of sorrowful spirit. I have*
> *drunk neither wine nor intoxicating drink, but*
> *have poured out my soul before the Lord."*

Reread verse thirteen, "Now Hannah spoke in her heart; only her lips moved, but her voice was not heard." Then, when she was accused of being drunk, she replied, "[I] have poured out my soul before the Lord."

Friend, make no mistake: a prayer prayed within one's heart is just as much heard and significant as one prayed with one's audible voice. God hears your *heart* as much as He hears the words coming from your mouth.

Have you ever felt at a loss for words to effectively communicate how you were feeling? You know, that time when you were so deeply hurt you couldn't seem to muster up the words to articulate it? That time it seemed no words in the English language could do it justice? Even in those times, He hears your heart. If you ever go to God in prayer and simply cannot find the words to say, know that He hears your heart. I cannot count the times I've told the Lord I just couldn't find the right words but asked Him to instead read my heart and then trusted He did just that.

He is capable of it. He alone.

You don't have to do anything to gain His attention—you've already got it! There's no appointment needed. He doesn't keep bankers' hours, and He is even available on holidays!

From the earliest morning hour to the latest hour of the day.

Every minute of every hour.

Every day of every week.

Every month of every year.

5
He Is Near You

*I will not forget you. See, I have engraved
you on the palms of My hand.*

—Isa. 49:15–16

LEAH'S THIRD SON was named Levi. Levi means
"to be joined or attached." I'd have to say that out of all
these names, this one seems to grip my heart the most.
There's just something about not feeling connected
with someone you love.

Women especially have a deep need to feel connected
to others. There's something within us that is unsettled

if that connection is missing. This unsettling feeling often sends us on a quest to find it. This kind of connection isn't just experienced in a marriage—even though it is quite powerful within that context. Women also want to feel connected to friends. While we cannot feel this connection with every person in our lives, we can experience it with those who are closer than others. Jesus was definitely closer to the disciples than the crowds of people He encountered on a daily basis.

I've sat across from several women who have shared how lonely they are. Feelings of isolation and a lack of connectivity cause so many wounds in the hearts of women. Women were created differently from men in this need. Men aren't asking one another to meet for coffee at the local Caribou to share their feelings. Women fill coffee shops, sometimes for hours (yes, I've been one of them!), sharing hearts and making connections with friends. Somehow, once we finally give up our table for another set of friends looking to make their own connections, we feel refreshed and encouraged. A connection has been made!

Just this week Tim traveled to another state for work, and I had a couple of friends over. The weather was gorgeous, and as we visited the time just went by so fast. We laughed, shared tender moments, and prayed with one another.

Women are more relational. We love to hear about all the details and are thrilled to share! We are able to interrupt our friend to gain more details while said friend never skips a word. I'm sure you can understand (and may even be nodding your head as you're reading) the very real need you and I have to feel connected.

So, what if it's lacking? Coming back to the lives we've been looking at, Jacob clearly was not connected to Leah. It lacked in his thoughts, words, and actions. Yet, as we've seen in the case of the sons before, God remained faithful. God was very near to Leah.

How are your connections? Are you in a desperate place that has you tempted to be joined in an unhealthy relationship because, well, it's better than nothing? These relationships can be friends or boyfriends or a combination of both. Sadly, I've seen women take an unhealthy dating relationship to the next step—marriage—knowing it's not the best choice. For reasons that run pretty deep within her heart, she just cannot separate herself from that man.

I once had a membership at a local gym that often had music playing throughout every room. Once I walked through the front door, it could be heard, but it hadn't always been that way. I'm not certain, but there may have been a management change, and that was the result. You maybe can read a tone into my words that would lead you to think I wasn't real thrilled with the music selection.

You'd be spot on.

Not only was it louder than I thought was reasonable, the songs were very offensive to me as a woman. One cannot miss the words to some of the songs playing. On one particular morning, the songs on the playlist included a man singing about his girlfriend. The lyrics included such repulsive words that I won't include them here. In addition, she was referred to as "stupid because she keeps coming back."

When I think of the age group of young girls (and maybe women, I suppose) listening to this type of music, I am saddened. It's being played on their iPods, on the school bus, and at the school dance. What's even sadder is that if we as parents aren't speaking into the lives of our daughters and granddaughters about how beautiful they are—make no mistake—they will hear the opposite somewhere.

Our daughters and granddaughters need to hear of their value and worth in Christ. We should never leave it up to the culture and social media.

The type of ministry to which God has called me often puts me across from women who are deeply wounded. I've had many women share raw decisions they've made because they wanted love and to be connected—decisions that still affect their lives.

The motives for which we do the things we do are a reflection of a greater need.

I encourage you to reread that and let it sink in a bit. I don't say that with any tone of condemnation. Far from it. I say that with love and from experience. My past is full of decisions...compromises that I later regretted. If I were sitting across from you, I'd put my arm around you and reassure you that I get it. I know how our desperate search for connection leads us down a slippery slope.

I would hand you a Kleenex (and probably use one myself) and begin to speak into your life. I'd first tell you, given that you've already made a decision for Jesus Christ, that He is living in you. (If you hadn't made that decision to follow Christ, we'd start there by praying together and inviting Him into your heart.) Galatians 2:20 tells us, "but Christ lives in me." He has *chosen* to live within *you*. That Jesus Christ is fully alive within you gives you such value and worth. He's abiding in *you*. The King! He has found you and me worthy of making our hearts a dwelling place for Himself. Incredible.

Just as God was very near to Leah, He is just as near to you! God will never betray you; He is fully committed to you and will never walk out on you.

Ever.

Listen to His words:

But now, thus says the Lord, who created you, Oh Jacob, and He who formed you, O Israel: "Fear not for I have redeemed you; I have called you by your name; you are Mine. When you pass through the waters, I will be with you; and through the rivers, they shall not overflow you. When you walk through the fire, you shall not be burned, nor shall the flame scorch you. Fear not, for I am with you."

—Isa. 43:1–2, 5

Can a mother forget the baby at her breast and have no compassion on the child she has borne? Though she may forget, I will not forget you! See, I have engraved you on the palms of My hands.

—Isa. 49:15–16

I will never leave you nor forsake you.

—Heb. 13:5

Before I end this chapter, I want to tell you that you deserve to be surrounded with people who will encourage, support, and value you as a human being.

You deserve to be loved well, cared for deeply, and esteemed. You deserve to have relationships that speak words of life over you.

I'm in no way suggesting you separate from your husband. Trust me when I say God can bring change in a marriage. What I am saying is that we need to be careful about whom we are either seeking a relationship with or are currently involved in.

Leah gave herself—all of herself—to Jacob. God brought her through that desperate time in her life and gave her a great testimony, one that we as women can still glean much from. People aren't perfect, and from time to time those we hold dear hurt us. Over the years I've been hurt by close friends and family, but God worked things out—usually within me first.

As I type this chapter, I cannot help but think about the countless women who gave all of themselves to their spouse. When they walked down the aisle and said the words *I do*, they meant it forever, and then one day, something changed within their husband. I'll be addressing this in another chapter, but please know deep within your heart and soul that God sees you. God hears you. God is near to you.

Of great note, if you are currently in an abusive relationship, I strongly encourage you to seek guidance and counsel. God never condones abuse.

Ever.

6
The Shift

This time I will praise the Lord.

—Gen. 29:35

YOU'VE PROBABLY HEARD the phrase "I had a lightbulb moment." It describes that moment when, after much confusion, something just clicks in our brains, and all of sudden, a connection is made in our thoughts.

As I mentioned in a previous chapter, I'm sort of directionally challenged. If I have to venture out into an area that is unfamiliar to me without my husband, we go over directions several times until that ah-ha moment takes place. Usually it takes place once he tells me of a certain restaurant or mall or other significant object near my destination.

Just as there's a moment when I make a connection in my thoughts about where I'm driving to, there's often a connection that takes place in our thoughts and hearts when we understand something in Scripture in a fresh way. It's usually at these times that we see and understand God in a fuller way, a way that draws us closer to Him. It fuses our faith and spurs us on.

Genesis 29:35 records a shift that took place in Leah's thoughts and heart. See if you can catch it.

"She conceived again, and when she gave birth to a son she said, 'This time I will praise the Lord.' So she named him Judah. Then she stopped having children."

Did you catch it? Leah finally looked to God for His love and approval. Her expectation was placed where it should be: in the One who would never disappoint. I think we even see this in the name she chose for her fourth son. Judah means "praise."

Something shifted in Leah. "This time…" When she came to a place where she could come to terms that what she was seeking in another could only be fully experienced in God, she must've felt such a relief from burden. Leah spent most of her life striving for what we all crave, only to be disappointed. Boy, would I love to sit across the table from Leah at the local Starbucks and pick her brain!

This time.

What possibly could have caused such a paradigm shift in Leah's thinking that she said, "This time I will praise the Lord"? Was it that she had grown tired of unmet expectations of Jacob? Was she weary of disappointment? Was it that she had grown frustrated with herself that she kept making herself vulnerable to being hurt? We do that, you know. We get frustrated with ourselves, and if we're not careful, it can lead us to self-condemnation.

Do you remember earlier in the book when I talked about not misplacing power? The moment Leah made a decision that *this time* she was going to do something different, she gave power to her God.

Every single day, you and I are presented with choices. Can I ask you, is there an area of your life that you wished was different? Because we're talking about our identity in Christ in this book, is there an area in which you feel like you just cannot gain freedom? While we're going to start digging deeper into exactly what our identity is in the next chapter, I don't want you to miss how powerful those words—*this time*—are. Here's the thing: even though a situation may not change right away, or the person who's treating us poorly hasn't changed, that doesn't mean *we* can't.

The moment you and I make a choice to look unto God and receive everything He wants to give us and walk confidently in His truth is the moment a shift takes place in our lives. It's going to take time, effort, and determination, but it's possible.

In the final chapter of this book, I'm going to give you a few key ways to keep your expectation in God. Walking through this life as a confident woman is possible, even for you! No matter what your past looks like, what station of life you're currently in, what your bank account looks like, whether you graduated from high school, or whether you're young or old, it's possible because He said it is. Deuteronomy 30:19 admonishes, "therefore choose life."

The power of choice! It's incredible!

And in God's faithfulness, He will give you and me the strength and courage to make that choice for life each and every time. We just need to ask and believe!

Can I ask you another question? Is what you're doing—your thoughts and behaviors—working for you? Are they giving you the results you want? Can I humbly suggest, from one who has been there too many times to count, that you stop what isn't working?

My goodness, I have spent so many years miserable...I don't make that suggestion with any tone of condemnation. Can you in your mind's eye visualize two metal shackles around your ankles? Not only are those things heavy, but they limit the mobility of the person who's wearing them. Galatians 5:1 gives us some pretty good news: "So Christ has truly set us free." It is for freedom that Christ has set us free! I can see Him bending down with the keys to those shackles and unlocking them. We have a role in that; it's our job to lift our feet out of them.

They're unlocked, my friend. Now step out of them, and begin to walk freely!

There's such freedom when we no longer seek in others what only God can give. That freedom is not only felt by us but by those we've put those expectations upon. I've been on both sides of this cycle. I've been the one seeking and therefore put unrealistic expectations on my friends and family. I've also been the one on whom unrealistic expectations have been placed. I know I've disappointed friends and family because, for whatever reason, I couldn't be what they needed at the moment.

When people on both sides of this cycle stop looking at one another and instead lift their eyes to the One who can satisfy every need, everyone wins. Everyone is set free.

So I'm sure you're asking, "Does that mean we should never expect our spouses, friends, and families to show love and support?" My one-word answer is *no*! We just need to keep perspective.

God wants us to be so confident in who we are in Him and in His love for us that no matter what happens, who says what, who doesn't say or doesn't do, I've got my confidence in Him alone. If I were sitting across from you, I'd openly share with you that I don't always feel supported and encouraged. I'm always hopeful that those in my life will express kindness and encouragement, but it doesn't always happen.

So what are we supposed to do? How does one react to that? We have a choice at that given moment: we either fall to pieces and continue to walk around in our insecurities, or we make a choice to love those in our lives regardless, and we find what we need in Christ alone.

In the fall of 2015, I hosted the first annual She Rises women's conference. It was a dream God put within me some time ago, and 2015 would be the year I'd see that dream become reality. When that dream was first placed in my heart all those years ago, I shared it with those closest to me. Friends stood with me in prayer and encouragement, believing in me when I didn't believe in myself. Fast-forward to 2015 and the launching of She Rises, when with anticipation I shared the exciting news and was taken aback by some of the responses.

While I've been in ministry for thirteen years, I knew God was calling me to walk on some uncharted waters, trusting He was leading each step. I was nervous but wanted to be obedient. I felt myself at the crossroads I described above. I had a choice to make. Would I allow myself to be discouraged and the lack of support to deter me, or would I refocus, pull up my waders, and walk on that water regardless? For those of you unfamiliar with what waders are, they are high, waterproof boots used for wading. Mine would be colorful, of course!

I find such strength and courage when I read the story of Nehemiah. He was such a man of great character and determination. He displays a confidence, not only in what he believed God had called him to do but a solid confidence in who he was in God. As you read this incredible book of the Bible and get to chapter four, you see Nehemiah leading even when opposition is mounting. There's one word that almost makes me want to run a lap around the house. It's found in verse nine: *Nevertheless.*

Nehemiah was so confident in His God that even when the opposition was gaining momentum (compare chapter two), he placed his expectation in God alone.

Nevertheless.

I have had a "nevertheless" moment—a few of them, if I am completely honest. Those decisions have been defining for me, and they will be for you too. I don't know where you are in this whole confidence area of life, but what I do know is when I choose to follow where God is leading, it's always the best choice. He will forever and always lead us to a place of confidence in Him. Anything opposite of confidence is burdensome.

It's the heart of God to lead us to freedom—in every area of life.

7
Reclaiming Our Identity

Therefore if anyone is in Christ, he is a new creation; old things have passed away; behold, all things have become new.

—2 Cor. 5:17

WE'RE ALL AWARE that there's a great emphasis on protecting our identity in today's world. Companies go to great lengths to ensure consumers' information is protected. When there's a breach in that protection, it gets a great deal of attention in the media. At the workplace, measures are put in place to keep employees from downloading items to computers, visiting certain sites, and so forth, all in an effort to maintain security. We even take precautions in our homes. While I'm not the most tech-savvy gal around, I do know there's a name for that protection: firewall.

We have an even greater identity to be aware of. It's our identity in Christ. We cannot earn it and don't deserve it, but we've been given this identity because of the work on the Cross.

Our world is in constant change, and there's quite a bit of uncertainty in our world. It seems every morning we awake to something that changed overnight. It almost feels unavoidable, but even if those changes get a little too close to home, we can have a confident trust in the One who promises to never change. Hebrews 13:8 puts it this way: "Jesus Christ is the same yesterday and today and forever."

He'll never change His mind about you—ever.

He'll never degrade you, humiliate you, abuse your trust, or manipulate you—ever.

Because He never changes, you and I can have complete confidence that our identity—who *He* says we are—will never change.

The Word of God is the foundation for right thinking. Whenever I meet one-on-one with other women to help them overcome a situation, I always say, "Tell me about your devotional time." I'm not trying to be nosy or to make the precious one sitting across from me feel condemned. I want to get an idea of where the Word has a place in her life. The Word is packed with truth that sets us free, shows us who Jesus is, is the heart-beat of God, reproves us, challenges us, helps us gain wisdom—just to name a few.

We have to replace our old ways of thinking about ourselves with the truth found only in Scripture if we're going to be set free and stay free.

For this section I'm going to list very specific truths of who we are in Christ—truths I strongly feel are appropriate for this book. Again, this list is not exhaustive but will give you a great start. I encourage you to dive headlong into the Word and uncover these truths for yourself. I cannot stress enough how vital it is to read your Bible. These truths are a very real part of who you are; they are a part of your DNA!

Righteousness in Christ. Second Corinthians 5:21: "For He made Him who knew no sin to be sin for us, that we might become the righteousness of God in Him."

This means you and I have been made right with God. Jesus took upon Himself our sin, shame, guilt, and every shortcoming, for the sole purpose of making a way for every person on the face of the planet to come unashamedly before a holy and righteous God.

Jesus took our place. He took everything that we deserved and bore it for us instead. Jesus was sinless in every way yet became sin for us, for God imputed our sins upon Him.

What a demonstration of love!

Think of it: our God wants you and me close to Him. He wants a relationship with us, not a long-distance-type relationship, but a close, intimate relationship where we could come before Him unhindered by what we did wrong. Yes, there's repentance, and we'll talk about that, but I'm talking about what Jesus did for you and me to make us right in the eyes of God.

Because this is a part of our identity in Christ, we can move toward God, not be kept from Him. God declares believers in Christ righteous, in the sense of acquitting us, and He imparts righteousness to us.

Forgiven. 1 John 1:9: "If we confess our sins, He is faithful and just to forgive us our sins and to cleanse us from all unrighteousness."

Tell me, sweet friend, what do you see when you look in the mirror? Do you see someone who knows they've asked God for forgiveness of something, and although you know He's forgiven you, you just cannot seem to forgive yourself?

It's human nature, isn't it? Trust me when I say I know this one really well. Here's the thing: we're well aware of what we did wrong, what that failure was, that choice we made, and we really don't need to enlist the help of others with our recollection of events. We already know!

We're the ones staring back at ourselves in the mirror.

I find such freedom in Micah 7:18–19: "Who is a God like You, pardoning iniquity and passing over the transgression of the remnant of His heritage? He does not retain His anger forever, because He delights in mercy. He will again have compassion on us, and will subdue our iniquities. You will cast all our sins into the depths of the sea."

He delights in mercy! He has compassion! He casts our sin into the depths of the sea! Yes, there may be consequences to whatever choice we made that later needed forgiveness, but consequences don't mean we haven't been forgiven.

There is no one like our God to forgive! You are pardoned! In His immense compassion and faithfulness, He has forgiven. I like to think of it this way: He has the best pitching arm around and threw those sins into the depths of the sea, and because He owns the sea, He put up a "No Fishing" sign. No fishing. In other words, there's no deep-sea diving after them!

No record. Repent, and it's done. Period. Never to be brought up again.

Ever.

So, go ahead. Why don't you forgive yourself?

Friend of God. John 15:15: "No longer do I call you servants, for a servant does not know what his master is doing; but I have called you friends, for all things I have heard from My Father I have made known to you."

I'm not sure what your experience has been in the friendship area of life. Maybe when you hear that word it brings up bad memories of middle school. I remember elementary school as a time when kids for the most part got along. Although I know kids can be pretty cruel, elementary-age kids don't seem to categorize other kids.

But middle school?

I'm not sure what happens during that summer between elementary and middle school, but when kids enter middle school, it's a whole new realm of making friends. For some, those that once were friends no longer look at you in the hallway, let alone sit with you at the lunch table. While for others, friends (using that term loosely in this context) only want to be friends when it's convenient for them or when no one else is around.

I call that a fair-weather friendship. Beautiful one, there is absolutely no way God could be fair-weather. He's fully committed to you and will stay by your side even on your worst day.

Even if everyone else walks out on you, you can be confident of this truth: He will never, ever walk out on you.

He's called *you* a friend.

Chosen. First Peter 2:9: "But you are a chosen generation, a royal priesthood, a holy nation, His own special people, that you may proclaim the praises of Him who called you out of darkness into His marvelous light."

Chosen. Did you know that God would choose you even if no one else would or even if you wouldn't choose yourself? Maybe you remember gym class in middle school when the teacher selected two captains for a particular game. The rest of the class lined up, and the captains picked who they wanted on their team based on personality or athleticism. It's such an awkward feeling.

Were you like me, hoping that you'd be the next one chosen? Were you secretly hoping you wouldn't be the last one standing? It's embarrassing, humiliating, diminishing, and it definitely chips away at one's confidence.

Were you the one who was left standing? Were you the one who was picked last, knowing the only reason you were picked is because you had to go somewhere?

I was.

I wasn't really athletic, and I definitely didn't have the "right name," if you know what I mean. Choosing teams in gym class is almost like a popularity contest. I remember when I was finally picked. I remember feeling like I wasn't chosen because I was going to be an asset to the team.

Rather, when I was chosen, it sort of looked like this: it was usually between me and some other poor soul who was feeling as embarrassed as I was. The captain whose turn it was would, with a low voice and somewhat of a slouch (making it known I wasn't really wanted), call my name. There was no skip in my step as I approached the team, nor was I greeted with a high-five by my new teammates.

Brutal.

I know women who have gone to great lengths to be sure that doesn't happen in their adult lives. You maybe even know a few—women who have made choices to make sure they are noticed and stand a little taller in the eyes of others.

Chosen one, God would choose you, hands down.

Every. Single. Time.

He never does a lineup to select the right one based on any merit. Not quite convinced? Take a look at Colossians 1:12: "Giving thanks to the Father who has qualified us to be partakers of the inheritance of the saints in the light." Then just for extra measure, take a look at 2 Corinthians 3:5–6: "Not that we are sufficient of ourselves to think anything as being from ourselves, but our sufficiency is from God, who also made us sufficient."

Qualified and *sufficient*.

Those words describe you!

You *are enough!*

Accepted. Ephesians 1:6: "He has made us accepted in the Beloved."

Tim has worked in the metal-manufacturing field for close to twenty-five years. While I have never worked in the plant, I know enough to carry myself in a conversation simply because of his years of experience and living under the same roof. One area of the plant is known as the QA department—quality assurance. It's the department that looks over each piece prior to shipping to be sure everything has been done properly and according to standards set forth by the company.

For example, in the paint department, if even the slightest blemish is spotted on an item that was painted, it is rejected and sent back. In other words, the company wants to take every measure to ship quality items to the customer.

Accepted one, do you know God hasn't rejected you? In the example above, that department is looking for any flaws in the finished product. When God created you, He created you a masterpiece.

Unique.

He placed gifts and talents within you. If we think there's a possibility of being rejected, we fail to remember what He said in Psalm 139:13–15: "For You formed my inward parts; You covered me in my mother's womb. I will praise You for I am fearfully and wonderfully made; marvelous are Your works, and that my soul knows very well." God didn't create a flawed image when He created you. You are not flawed or rejected, but accepted! Right now. No need to get yourself together before you can come to Him. He accepts you now—quirks and all.

A relationship with Jesus isn't a popularity contest, with the most talented getting picked. There are no auditions or favorites. You don't have to earn His love or acceptance.

Ever.

One more thought about being accepted. If you're reading this and part of your story is that you were given up for adoption, and it's left you with questions about rejection, I want to give you a promise straight from the Word of God: "When my father and mother forsake me, then the Lord will take care of me" (Ps. 27:10).

Rejection runs deep into our souls, but it's not too deep that the healing power of Jesus can't go deeper still.

Blameless. Ephesians 1:4: "that we should be holy and without blame before Him."

Our culture has engaged in what I refer to as the Blame Game. It would appear people have become quick to point to others, often publicly, placing blame for decisions that weren't necessarily made with wisdom. While I do think anyone in a leadership position bears a considerable amount of responsibility, a responsibility to make wise decisions that are in the best interests of those he or she is leading, it appears our culture has put a "shame on you" spin on comments.

The unfortunate and very sad part of this new direction of our culture is that it has somehow reached our church pews and pulpits. It's in our families for as far back as some of us can remember. When I think of blame as it applies to our culture, I think of someone pointing a finger at another with a condemning tone and seasoned with shame.

Nowadays, many people find pleasure in making another look bad in others' eyes in a sheer effort to make themselves look better or feel better. You know—if eyes are looking and fingers are pointed in another direction, it definitely takes the focus off the individual placing blame.

Again, I am not talking about people in positions of leadership who are making ungodly decisions. Rather, I am talking about the trend in our culture that has grown incredibly shame-based.

The opposite of blameless is guilty. When Jesus bore our sins, He removed any blame or guilt. In Him He has presented you as blameless, without judgment or fault. If you are in Christ and have asked for forgiveness of sin, you are forgiven.

God's character isn't shame-based. He'll never point a finger at you and say, "Shame on you."

Ever.

Brought Near. Ephesians 2:13: "But now in Christ Jesus you who once were far off have been brought near by the blood of Christ."

Most everyone reading this book has been with someone who made you feel like you were boring. You know, those moments when the person you are with seems more interested in their cell phone, TV, or newspaper than you.

You are so loved by God that He wants you close—very close, in fact. You have been brought so near that you can feel His heartbeat and hear His whisper. He'll never keep you at arm's length, and He's not just tolerating you.

God never pushes us away as if He's somehow disgusted or disappointed in us.

He'll never grow tired of you, and you'll never be traded for something newer.

Ever.

Redeemed. Ephesians 1:7: "In Him we have redemption through His blood, the forgiveness of sins, according to the riches of His grace."

If you are in Christ, He has redeemed you and has given you freedom from the penalty, bondage, and power of sin. This is given because of Jesus's work on the Cross and Resurrection from the dead.

I was once at a gathering where, as a part of the service, we were asked to recite that we were in bondage to sin. Yes, we all are born with a sinful nature, but once we accept Jesus as our Lord and Savior, the bondage of sin is removed. The penalty of sin—separation from God—has been removed because He has purchased you back from having to receive that penalty.

You are freed from the power of sin in your life. While we are on this side of heaven, we will continue to sin and fall short of God's glory, but through Christ we now have forgiveness. That doesn't mean we keep on sinning just because we know we'll be forgiven. To do so would cheapen grace. It means that in Him we find the strength to overcome the power of it in our lives. Again, it all comes back to the finished work of the Cross and Resurrection. He removed the power of sin so it no longer has power over us!

Redemption never changes.

Ever.

Complete. Colossians 2:10: "You are complete in Him who is the head of all principality (rule and authority) and power" (clarification mine).

There's a stigma in our culture that tells women they will feel complete when they graduate from college, get married, have children, and work up the ladder to CEO.

Several years ago I had a conversation with a woman who, due to health concerns, had been advised to have a hysterectomy. Along with other symptoms, she had suffered for many years with excruciating pain. She sought the advice of a well-known OB/GYN who was highly respected in his field.

After much conversation and attempts with alternative approaches, she and her husband finally came to the decision that a full hysterectomy was her only recourse. This woman went on to tell me about how a couple of her friends made comments that she would be incomplete because she would no longer have the female organs to bear children.

One comment in particular haunted her for several years. A friend told her, "Women are incomplete without a uterus and ovaries. I just don't understand how women could have a hysterectomy and still feel like a woman." As if that wasn't enough, this friend added, "Hysterectomies just take away womanhood. I would never do that."

Quite a statement, huh?

Instead of getting support and understanding, this woman was left to feel incomplete. There are countless women in our world who are unable to have children biologically. Many choose adoption. Is a woman who chooses adoption any less woman—any less complete—because she for reasons outside her control was unable to give birth to a child?

The simple answer is no!

It's the same principle for those women who are unmarried. Culture would say there must be something wrong with her that no man wants to marry her. I have many single friends who either have chosen not to marry or whose husbands have passed away and they chose not to remarry. These women are strong, capable, and gifted. They have just as much potential and purpose as those women who are married.

How about the stigma of being a college graduate? Boy, that's a big one in today's culture. Our culture would tell us that what's most important isn't your work ethic, dedication to your employer, respect to management, or being on time each workday. No, our culture would tell us that what's important is how many degrees we have behind our names and titles before our names.

I have many friends who decided not to attend college yet are fulfilling positions with excellence. These women are incredible assets to their companies.

Don't miss my point. The above examples are only given because of their relevance in our culture. In no way am I suggesting that the desire to be married, have children, attend a college, or earn a degree is bad and should not be included in your life. I have all of those in my life. What I am saying is that so often we let things define whether or not we are complete.

The sheer number of women who have told me they got married because they "just didn't think [they] could live without a husband" is astonishing—not to mention the number of women who stay in college for way too long, earning degree after degree, because it satisfies something that is lacking within them.

Friend, God says you are complete *in* Him. It isn't a relationship or any one thing that makes us complete. It's Him.

Read it again: "you are complete in Him." It reads *"in Him."* In other words, God has created us complete in Him, having no deficiencies. Please don't misunderstand me; I am not talking about our sinful nature. Romans 3:23 clearly points out that "for all have sinned and fall short of the glory of God."

We as women just need to strike balance. Balance that says, "In Christ alone I am made complete; it isn't another person that makes me complete or any one thing." Balance that says, "Even if I'm currently not dating, not married, don't have children, or decide not to pursue a college degree, that doesn't make me any less complete than the woman sitting next to me who has one or all of those."

Of course you can flip those scenarios and apply them to some cultures that tell women they *have* to date in order to find a husband, that they *have* to have children, or that they *have* stay home and raise those children and not pursue an education.

Our completeness and wholeness is found in Him and Him alone!

8
Loyal Love

We love Him because He first loved us.

—1 John 4:19

LOVE. IT'S SUCH a common word in our everyday conversations. We use it to describe our affection for everything from our favorite drink at the local Starbucks to the shoes we just bought. We love our dogs, cats, new hairstyles, the latest technology devices, and food at our favorite restaurants.

Dare I say our culture has cheapened the meaning of the word *love*?

This last part of our identity, being loved, is so vital to us as followers of Christ that I've devoted an entire chapter to it. In my opinion, it's the foundation for everything else. Take a look at the following verses. Take a few minutes to meditate on them and let them sink into the depths of your soul.

> *Beloved, let us love one another, for love is of God.*
>
> —*1 John 4:7*

> *For God is love.*
>
> —*1 John 4:8*

> *This is real love—not that we loved God, but that He loved us and sent His Son as a sacrifice to take away our sin.*
>
> —*1 John 4:10*

Real love. We were created for real love, created to both receive and offer real love. In fact, there was something created within each of us—man, woman, and child—to have this real love, so much so that we will search for it in a plethora of ways. It's built within us, and there's no getting around it.

As I mentioned in an earlier chapter, the material in this book can be applied to men and women. However, I will direct this chapter toward women, but if you're a man reading this book, I trust you will be able to apply the truths contained within this chapter.

Women especially are created for love. It is our deepest need, even more than respect, honor, position, or esteem, we want to know love—*real love*. Dr. Emerson Eggerichs, in his DVD curriculum, *Love and Respect*, shares an incredible finding. Dr. Eggerichs shares that "if you went to your favorite store and stood in the card aisle, you'd find that most cards for women have some type of language that includes the word *love*."

However, if you scan the cards for men, you'll notice they often refer to his work, relaxing, or sadly, how inept they are at basic life skills. I won't even get into that subject.

The point I'm trying to make is that women have a different need than men in the area of love. Do men need love? Absolutely! Do men ever feel unloved? Absolutely! Is love their greatest need? Not necessarily. In that same DVD series, Dr. Eggerichs goes on to share that men's "greatest need is respect," respect as men and how God created them. Again, Dr. Eggerichs says, "The differences in how men and women were created aren't wrong; they're just different."

I don't want to get off-topic from the purpose of this book, but I do want to encourage you that if you'd like to learn more about love and respect as it relates to men and women, especially within the context of marriage, I recommend the *Love and Respect* series by Dr. Emerson Eggerichs. You can find his resources online. Both Tim and I would highly recommend this material and can give testimony of seeing it work in marriages to bring healing and forgiveness as well as an understanding of the needs of one another.

Coming back to the purpose of this chapter—real love—a woman will go to great lengths in a quest to find it. That quest can lead her into unhealthy relationships and making decisions that chip away her worth and value. Have you ever known someone who settled for a relationship with a significant other even though she was well aware it wasn't healthy?

Could you tell just by observation that she wasn't happy? Could you hear in various remarks that she didn't feel loved? Perhaps she has shared with you what happens behind closed doors that leads you to believe she's not living with real love.

I've sat across from too many women to count who have shared with me their disappointment with the lack of real love in their relationships—authentic love, genuine, through the highs and lows, and in sickness and health. Real love—no matter if we gain a few pounds, start seeing gray hairs, and things start to sag. Real love that supports, encourages, esteems, lifts up, believes in, is loyal, wants to spend time with us, and places more value on the relationship than his work and friends and colleagues.

I've sat across from too many women to count who have shared with me their stories of abuse, adultery, and pornography. I've heard too many stories of women who've heard the words "I don't think I love you anymore." I've heard too many stories of women who've heard the words "I don't think I *ever* loved you."

What about these stories:

"I am going to find my biblical wife."
"You've gotten so heavy."
"You're no fun anymore."
"Let's start watching these videos before having sex; it will be fun."

I've offered too many Kleenex to precious women who were shedding tears over how the men they were with suddenly changed. Too many times I've heard women admit that they know they deserve better. Too many times I've asked the question, "Have you talked to your husband (or boyfriend) about how you feel?" Too many times I've been given an answer full of reasons to excuse away the behavior of husbands or boyfriends.

It's always very interesting to me when I begin speaking words of life over that precious woman. Words that affirm and esteem her. She sits up a little taller and even shows a smile. The response I see when I tell her she deserves to be loved well, cared for deeply, and esteemed convinces me that we are created to receive it.

Before I go any further, I want to be sure you know that I am in no way telling you to leave your husband. I've mentioned it earlier, and I'll say it again: God can heal and restore marriages. There isn't a marriage out there that is beyond His restoring power. What I would recommend you do is surround yourself with trusted friends you can confide in, friends you know will stand with you, believing in God for change. Confide in your pastor so he or she knows how to support and pray for you. Go to your local bookstore or library to find resources from Christian authors on strength and courage and marriage. Of course, your Bible is a daily must.

Again, I know I've also mentioned this earlier, but if you are currently in an abusive relationship, please find wise counsel. God never approves of abuse.

Ever.

What I want to effectively convey in this chapter is that there's a love that's pure, right, faithful, and genuine. It won't abuse your trust or manipulate you. It's a real love, and it's found in Jesus Christ.

You maybe have had a great experience in receiving real love from another. That's great, and I rejoice with and for you! I've been in relationships that have been pretty unhealthy and in a very healthy relationship with my husband for over twenty-five years. I've seen and experienced both sides. Tim has been such a great example of what love looks like and feels like and how freely it should be given. He loves me genuinely and has never been hesitant to express it to me or our daughter. As wonderful as he is and as incredibly grateful as I am for him and for his daily expression of love, it still doesn't compare to the love I find in Christ. There is no earthly relationship that can compare.

Not one.

God has used Tim in my life, however. Through Tim, I have understood what healthy and unhealthy love look like, what faithfulness and commitment look like. Even when I have days when maybe my words aren't seasoned with grace, I get up on the wrong side of the bed, my attitude isn't stellar, or when it's getting harder to cover those grays (I *love* my stylist!), Tim is as steady as they come. I often describe him as "Steady Eddie." He just isn't given to emotions, and I don't have to worry about whether his feelings toward me will ever change.

I didn't always have that confidence, though. By the time Tim came into my life, I had been through a string of very unhealthy relationships. You know the song

"Looking for Love in All the Wrong Places"? Just in case you don't, let me share the chorus with you:

> I was lookin' for love in all the wrong places
> Lookin' for love in too many faces
> Searching their eyes, lookin' for traces
> Of what I'm dreamin' of
> Hopin' to find a friend...
> (Written by Wanda Mallette, Bob Morrison,
> and Patti Ryan. Sung by Johnny Lee)

That song could have been written for me. I hungered for love. I have a long list of ways I desperately searched for it. By the time Tim came into my life, I had major trust and self-worth issues. Yet God used Tim to tear down, brick by brick, the walls I built around my heart so that real love could find its way in.

I like what God says about this heart transformation in Ezekiel 36:26: "I will give you a new heart and put a new spirit within you; I will take the heart of stone out of your flesh and give you a heart of flesh." Friend, no matter what your experience has been, there is a love that is real. If you don't know Jesus Christ, can I encourage you to turn to the end of this book and pray the simple prayer of salvation?

An often-quoted verse is John 3:16: "For God so loved the world that He gave His only begotten Son, that whoever believes in Him should not perish but have everlasting life." Sin originated hundreds of years ago in the garden of Eden. If you're not familiar with the story of Adam and Eve, I encourage you to read Genesis 1–3.

Sin separates us from a holy God and no one on the planet is excusable. Without a Savior we would never be able to confidently approach God because He is holy; we are not. Every person is born with a sin nature. We needed a Savior who would cover our sin. God saw that need, and because of His immeasurable love for you and me, He sent His Son, Jesus, to take our place on the Cross. He bore the sin, shame, judgment, and condemnation we deserved. Why? Because He loves you.

You.

Even if you were the only person walking the face of the planet, God would have still seen you and sent Jesus to die for you. Why? Because He loves you.

You.

Take a few minutes and let that go down deep. God sent His Son for you. Just typing those words gives me pause. In my unworthiness and sinfulness, Jesus came for me. Jesus came for you. Jesus came for the world. It is because of His great sacrifice on the Cross and then Resurrection (see John 20) that we can believe we are everything He says we are.

Why? Because He paid the price.

I Do…Forever

When you read the words "I do," does it make you think of your wedding day? I wanted to talk to those who married Mr. Right and to those who'd admit that Mr. Right wasn't all that "right"; you knew he had a few things to work on, but it seemed he was giving effort to change. After all, don't we all have areas needing improvement?

Only, at some point he decided this marriage wasn't for him anymore. Have you been the one who heard those words "I don't love you anymore"? Are you the one who was left with the kids, the mortgage, and the single life, while the one you married ran off with the one he "loves"?

The sting of betrayal is sharp. After all, when you went to the altar and said those words, "I do," you meant it for forever. You gave yourself heart and soul to this man. You gave your emotions to him and opened up to this man in ways you maybe hadn't before.

In a marriage there's an intimacy, not only physically but emotionally. This other person knows things about you that others may not know. You've trusted that person into your life, your dreams, your fears, your everything. Then, with one single decision, that trust and intimacy is broken. *Poof.* Just like that.

Read again 1 John 4:8: "God is love." It's who He is, and He cannot separate Himself from it. He created love, defines love, and sets the standard for what love looks like.

It always comes back to God's unchanging, unfailing, unconditional, and unending love for us. Always has. Always will. *You* are loved. He loves everything about you. He loves your name, the curve of your smile, the way you laugh, your body type, what excites you, etc.

God's love for you is a committed love. It will be constant through the highs and lows of life. His love will see you through dark hours and deep valleys. His love will celebrate with you and sit beside you to comfort you.

My friend, His love is loyal. He promises to never change. As a gentle reminder, let me put this promise in front of you: "Jesus Christ is the same yesterday, today, and forever" (Heb. 13:8).

9
Choosing (You)•nique

*I will praise You, for I am fearfully and
wonderfully made; marvelous are Your
works, and that my soul knows very well.*

—Ps. 139:14

DO YOU REMEMBER when we first sat down
together in chapter two, and I encouraged you to not
think that Jacob meant our husbands are the source of
your lack of confidence? I listed a few suggestions to
help you see that Jacob can represent anyone in our
lives. Since we've been sitting together for so long now,
would you grant me permission to ask you what may
seem like a difficult question?

Are *you* your own Jacob?

Hard question, I know. Friend, please don't read a tone into that question. I ask it with the pure motive to help you perhaps see another angle to insecurity. If it helps, I will be very honest with you and tell you that I know I have been my own Jacob, and if I'm not careful, I can be again. Being set free is one thing; maintaining freedom and living from that place is another. I have to be determined every single day.

Let me explain. When we're hurting and *feel* looked down upon by others, it's easy to cast blame on someone else. Confidence can easily be mistaken for pride. So often those who *seem* prideful are simply confident women. A confident woman carries herself differently and is often accused of thinking too highly of herself. Here's one clear-cut way to tell the difference:

> A confident woman who has placed her confidence in Christ is kind and offers a "leg up" to another. She's not threatened by another woman's gifts.

Women who have their confidence in themselves or things, on the other hand, feel threatened by another woman's gifts and refuse to offer a "leg up" because they fear attention may be given to the one they're helping instead of themselves. Remember reading why we do the things we do (wanting to be seen, heard, and noticed by others)?

If you'd admit, like me, that you've been your own Jacob in that you've compared yourself to another and, based on your comparison, decided you're not good enough, this chapter is for you.

Dr. Seuss asked, "Why fit in when you were born to stand out?"

While holding this book with one hand, open your other hand with your palm facing you. No one else on this planet has those same markings! No one else on this planet has *your* DNA! No one else on this planet has *your* fingerprint!

No one.

If being different from others was so bad, why would God create us with such distinctiveness? You were created in His image (Gen. 1:27)! He didn't create a mistake or look at you and think, "That'll have to do."

Remember what Jesus said in John 8:32: "You shall know the truth and the truth shall make you free." If you can see perhaps you're the Jacob in your life, let the truth set you free:

> There will always be someone who seems prettier than you.
> There will always be someone who seems more popular than you.

There will always be someone who seems more talented than you.

There will always be someone who seems more educated than you.

There will always be someone who seems thinner than you.

But there will only be *one you*.

Comparison is bait dangled by Satan in front of us to cause separation and division in the Body of Christ. It holds us back, keeps us offended, and ultimately limits our effectiveness in advancing the Kingdom in this world.

We need one another!

All of us!

We need *you*.

Ephesians 2:10 reads: "For we are His workmanship, created in Christ Jesus for good works, which God prepared beforehand that we should walk in them." Then listen to Psalm 139:14: "I will praise you for I am fearfully and wonderfully made; marvelous are Your works, and that my soul knows very well."

Do you see that you that are His workmanship and that His work is marvelous? He is the Master Designer! True, you may not have the same gifts someone else has—you may not be able to carry a tune or be the next gourmet chef—but you do have gifts! You do have something pretty spectacular to offer the Body of Christ and this world!

What can you do?

Do you like to teach others? Perhaps you should consider teaching Sunday school or a women's Bible study.

Do you like to write? Perhaps now is the time you sit down and start typing out those words.

Do you like serving? Perhaps you should look into finding ways to serve alongside your church.

Do you like to engage your community? Perhaps now is the time to see how you can help at the local homeless shelter, library, or elderly home.

Maybe you are the one who is gifted in the kitchen. Look for ways to use that gift to help others. Can you bring a plate of cookies or a meal to someone who's recovering from surgery or has recently experienced financial difficulties?

Maybe you are the one who can play an instrument or sing. Nursing homes are always looking for volunteers in their activity departments.

Are you crafty? Making something from home and blessing another with it is always rewarding.

How about sending cards to someone for no special reason other than just to say you're thinking about her?

What about visiting a shut-in?

Be the best door greeter! I bet the people at your church and possible visitors would enjoy and feel blessed by seeing your smile greet them on a Sunday morning.

How about taking a coworker out for lunch, just because?

Do you like to sew? Sew a few blankets for the church nursery. Make a few scarves or hats for the homeless shelter.

The list could go on and on, but I hope you can see there are numerous ways we can use our gifts to bless others. Advancing the Kingdom in the world doesn't always mean evangelism and standing in the pulpit. The above-mentioned ideas are very practical but speak volumes to others. By doing something for another, you are being an expression of God's love.

Just because what you're gifted in keeps you out of the limelight, never underestimate the impact it has on another's life.

Celebrate your uniqueness and stop wanting to be what someone else is because what they have or do seems more impactful or important.

Romans 12:4–5 puts it this way: "For as we have many members in one body, but all the members do not have the same function, so we, being many, are one body in Christ, and individually members of one another."

Yes, we're different, but we're created that way. You were created with purpose and unique gifts for the Kingdom! No longer use the differences you see between you and another woman as a measuring rod, but celebrate your uniqueness.

Together we're stronger. Together we're better. Together we can do more.

10
Keep Your Confidence On!

When Jesus heard him, he stopped and said, "Tell him to come here." So they called the blind man. "Cheer up," they said. "Come on, He's calling you!" Bartimaeus threw aside his coat, jumped up, and came to Jesus.

—Mark 10:49–50

HAVE I MENTIONED that I am a shopper? I like everything about it. From driving to the store, thinking about what great deal I might find, to thumbing through racks, to trying things on and just feeling fabric, I like to shop! I don't necessarily have to buy something for it to be considered a good shopping trip. I enjoy window shopping too.

Not too long ago, I made what was supposed to be an in-and-out trip to one of my favorite stores. I had had a full day, and before going home I needed to stop by the store for something to go along with the main dish I was serving for supper. I remember thinking while driving there and even as I was walking through the parking lot that this needed trip required me to focus on the task at hand. There was no time for shopping, not even a stroll through the department.

Eyes straight ahead. I purposely didn't even get a cart but instead picked up one of those shopping baskets that are stacked by the entrance door.

I made it to the grocery aisle I needed, and as I was approaching the checkout lane nearest the grocery side of the store, behold, the lines were so long I found myself standing by the lanes in the clothing section. As I walked that direction, the displays were simply adorable. The tables were arrayed with brilliant colors, and just one item suckered me in.

So, with my purse on one arm and the shopping basket on the other, I started thumbing through the rack. I really liked what I had seen, and although I didn't have time to try it on, I knew I could return it if it didn't fit.

To my amazement I could not find a hanger that had my size. Then, all it took was a small shift in focus—a lift of the head and eye—to notice I was standing in the maternity department! Believe me when I say there is no way this body is giving birth to another child! But it does make me wonder why they didn't have cute clothes like that when I was pregnant twenty-five years ago.

Ladies, just as something from the maternity wear doesn't fit me, and I'd look and feel not dressed right, our former ways of living insecurely don't fit us! There's nothing about that old wardrobe that makes us feel like empowered, strong, capable, and confident women. Confidence is what God wants you and me clothed in! And here's some great news! It's a one-size-fits-all—no need to try it on first or ask for an opinion about whether it looks okay. It'll fit you! God promises it! He's the best tailor in the business, and He's made it just right for you!

I want you to take a look at Mark 10:46–52, and then together we're going to unpack these verses:

> *Then they reached Jericho, and as Jesus and His disciples left town, a large crowd followed Him. A blind beggar named Bartimaeus (son of Timaeus) was sitting beside the road. When Bartimaeus heard Jesus of Nazareth was nearby, he began to shout, "Jesus, Son of David, have mercy on me!"*

"Be quiet!" many people yelled at him. But he only shouted louder, "Son of David, have mercy on me!" When Jesus heard him, He stopped and said, "Tell him to come here." So they called the blind man. "Cheer up," they said. "Come on, He's calling you!"

Bartimaeus threw aside his coat, jumped up, and came to Jesus.

"What do you want Me to do for you?" Jesus asked. "My Rabbi," the blind man said, "I want to see!" And Jesus said to him, "Go for your faith has healed you." Instantly the man could see, and he followed Jesus down the road.

Before I go any further, I just want to make sure you caught something that we started with ten chapters ago. Remember when we first started? We looked at how God sees, God hears, and God connects. Take a look at it again: "When Jesus heard Him, He stopped and said, 'Tell him to come here.'" All three of those points are contained in that one verse. Amazing!

In the days in which this story took place, men and women wore garments that were quite long. Most were ankle length, hovering just over the sandal strap. In today's current fashion, women can find long skirts that are lightweight, in a wide array of styles and colors.

I have a couple of them myself, and as much as I enjoy wearing them, I do have to give attention to the steps I make when using stairs. The skirts are just long enough that if I'm not careful, the bottom will get caught around the heel of my sandal. It has happened a time or two, and thankfully I have been spared the embarrassment (and bumps and bruises) of falling.

When Jesus called for Bartimaeus to come, it says he threw aside his coat. It makes me think that in his seated position, the garment he was wearing may have gotten caught around his ankle, keeping him from jumping up and going to Jesus. This verse paints such a vivid picture to me of a man not wanting anything to get in his way.

If you and I are going to live confidently, we have to cast off anything that would hinder us from doing so—things such as insecurity, self-loathing, self-shaming talk, hating oneself, a defeated mind-set, or doubt of anything we see as truth about our identity. Basically, anything that cannot be found in Scripture. It's all got to go.

Whatever the "label" is on the clothing you're wearing, if it's not empowering, equipping, and speaking words of life over you, it needs to go. Is it time for a new wardrobe?

Often in the Bible, our faith is compared to a runner running a race. You can find these verses in Isaiah

40:31, 1 Corinthians 9:24–26, Galatians 2:2, Philippians 2:16, Hebrews 12:1, and 1 Peter 4:4.

I like to run and have incorporated some form of running into my exercise routine for several years. Over the years, I've learned what works for me and what doesn't. One of the things that I avoid at all costs is carrying things or having things strapped to my waist. Many runners don't mind it all, but it just doesn't work for me. Carrying extra things makes me feel weighed down, and my focus seems to be on those items instead of what's in front of me.

However, there are days when I set out on an early-morning run and I leave the house with a light jacket. If you're familiar with running, you know that as your heart rate increases, so does your body temperature. Inevitably, it seems that not long into those runs, I want to remove the jacket. It's just getting in the way.

Just as there is careful thought given to what type of clothing runners wear while running, careful thought must be given to what you and I are "putting on" each and every day. While you're maybe getting a new wardrobe and now wearing your identity with confidence, remember this as you go through your day-to-day life:

Do not, therefore, fling away your fearless confidence, for it has a glorious and great reward.

—Heb. 10:35 (AMP)

There will be times in your life when some old way of thinking and seeing yourself will try to work its way back into your wardrobe. In this chapter I want to give you a few timeless tips to stay on course. Of course, you can't do this alone and in your own strength. Thank God He doesn't expect us to! I'm fully convinced that as you implement these into your life, you'll continue to grow and live confidently in this area!

Be a woman of the Word. The Word of God has the power to transform and renew our minds. It tells us what to think upon and what He thinks about us and our lives. The Bible alone has the power to change our thoughts. Numerous reading materials are out there that God does use in our lives, but above all, the Bible should be our first choice.

If we're not in the Word, how will we know what is the truth and what is a lie? Second Corinthians 10:5 tells us: "Casting down arguments and every high thing that exalts itself against the knowledge of God, bringing every thought into captivity to the obedience of Christ."

Our enemy, Satan, will stop at nothing to keep you and me bound to our past. Our freedom scares him. From time to time, he will drop thoughts in your mind and use others to discourage you (often unintentionally on their part), all in an effort to pull you back into bondage.

Listen to what Jesus refers to him as in John 8:44: "He (referring to Satan) was a murderer from the beginning, and does not stand in truth, because there is no truth in him. When he speaks a lie, he speaks from his own resources, for he is a liar and the father of it" (clarification mine).

Revelation 12:10 refers to Satan as the accuser of the brethren: "Then I heard a loud voice saying in heaven, 'Now salvation, and the kingdom of our God, and the power of His Christ have come, for the accuser of the brethren, who accused them before our God day and night, has been cast down.'" He stands accusing you and me.

When you find yourself thinking and/or feeling defeated, discouraged, worthless, and unloved, ask yourself if what you're thinking can be found in the Bible. If what you're thinking and/or feeling doesn't align with the truth of Scripture, then it's a lie.

Take hold of your thoughts; don't let them take hold of you.

Speak the Word out! Jesus is our greatest example. When He was tempted by Satan, He always replied, "It is written…" (see Matt. 4:4, 7, 10). Dig into the Word! If you're new in your faith or new to the discipline of reading your Bible, I recommend starting in the Gospels. The Gospel of John is always a great starting point. Commit a verse to memory—and then another.

If you were to come to my house on any given day, you'd find I have Scripture hanging up throughout my house. I have it taped to my bathroom mirror and refrigerator door; it's in my bedroom and family room. I have been known to put verses in my car. Scripture verses that are speaking to me in whatever season I am in currently. I look at them and repeat them throughout the day.

It may seem rather radical, and guests to our home may raise their eyebrows, but I am determined to have the Word in front of me at all times.

The battle for our thoughts is too real for me to not have the truth in me.

Testify! Revelation 12:11 reads, "And they overcame him by the blood of the Lamb (Jesus) and by the word of their testimony" (clarification mine). Who have we overcome? Satan and his schemes.

Jesus did a complete work on the Cross, leaving nothing undone. He was victorious in beating anything Satan could throw at us. Because He is victorious, if you are in Christ, you are victorious!

It's up to us as followers of Christ to appropriate that victory of the complete work on the Cross over our lives. One commentary puts it this way: "The church's constant posture under the authority of the Cross's victory by the blood of the Lamb and steadfastness to the promise and authority of God's Word—the word of their testimony—is the key to overcoming."

The key to overcoming.

Not only is this referring to the Church as whole, but it's also referring to you and me as those who make up the church.

Give testimony of what Jesus has done for you! Give testimony of how He has opened your eyes to understand the truth of your identity in Christ. Tell someone!

Be *that* woman! When I think of all the years I lived under a mantle of shame, regret, insecurity, and rejection, I often wonder: If another woman in the faith had come alongside me and spoken words of life over me, would it have taken me this long to be free?

I refuse to sit there and ponder that, but instead I have made up my mind to follow the wise words of Proverbs 31:26: "When she speaks, her words are wise, and she gives instructions with kindness" (NLT). I want to be a woman who looks for ways to give to others. I want to be a woman who is confident in who she is in Christ, not threatened by another's gifts because they may be different from mine.

I want to be a confident woman who looks for those coming up after me, the next generation, knowing that what He has done within me He wants do through me. I don't want the next generation to wait years to walk confidently in their identity in Christ. In all honesty, the world is in desperate need, and we simply don't have years to wait.

If the Kingdom is going to continue to advance on this earth, it's going to take an "all hands on deck" effort. It will take every one of us fulfilling our God-given purposes.

Be *that* woman you didn't have in your life but wished you did. Be the woman who seeks ways to help develop and speak into the lives of others. Be the woman whose heart is full of love and whose kindness is spoken from her mouth.

You have something to offer! You were created with and for a purpose! You have God-given potential!

I can't believe this book is coming to end. I feel like we've sat across from one another for quite a while now, but it's time—time to arise and go!

> *Arise, shine;*
> *For your light has come!*
> *And the glory of the Lord is risen upon you.*

> —*Isaiah 60:1*

Believing in and for each of you!
Susan

His Name Is Jesus

IF YOU FOUND this book in your hands and have never accepted Jesus Christ as your Lord and Savior, there's good news! You can, right now at this very moment! Right where you're sitting, you can pray the following and know without doubt that He hears you!

God, I admit I have sinned and have fallen short of your glory. I have made mistakes and am repenting of those. Please forgive me.

I believe You sent Your Son, Jesus, into the world. I believe He died on the Cross and rose three days later. I believe He is the Savior of the world.

I confess Jesus as my Lord and Savior. I want to live my life to bring You honor and glory. Please help me to do that.

If you just prayed that prayer, I encourage you to take the next step and tell someone! I encourage you to find a Bible-teaching church and get connected with a Bible study or small group for discipleship.

Notes

CHAPTER 8: LOYAL Love

1. Rev. Emerson Eggerichs, PhD. *Love and Respect.* Love and Respect Ministries, Inc. © 09/01/06 201 Monroe Ave. NW, Ste. 701 Grand Rapids, MI 49503 www.lovenandrespect.com.

Susan Vandenheuvel is passionate about helping women discover their fullest potential in Christ and realizing the freedom of seeing themselves through the eyes of their Creator, not the lens of their past.

Discovering these truths can be the catalyst that changes women's lives!

Susan is the Founder of She Rises in Minnesota. By teaching the uncompromising Word of God, the mission of She Rises is to see women of every age and background set free in every area of their lives and inspired to discover their God-given potential and purpose.

Susan is a pastor with the Assemblies of God and is often featured as a keynote speaker at women's events. She combines thirteen years of ministry with real-life experiences and is adept at connecting with her audience.

Susan lives with her husband, Tim, in central Minnesota.

For more information about Susan and her ministry, please visit www.sherisesmn.org.